THE MARRIAGE MANUAL FOR MEN
60 MINUTES TO A BETTER MARRIAGE

DEDICATION

I would like to dedicate this book to my wife and children. They have been very patient with me over the past 16 months while I regularly discussed the writing of this book.

You may be wondering how it could possibly take a year to write such a short book. Reread the above lines: I said they tolerated me discussing the need to finish the book, not me spending time away from them writing the book.

Finding the right balance between family, faith, friends, fun and finances is always a challenge in life. Each of us has our own hierarchy of choices by which we balance our sometimes-competing interests and responsibilities.

Thanks to my family for their support during the times when my scale tipped away from them as I worked on this book.

TABLE OF CONTENTS

WELCOME

Congratulations on purchasing your new marriage!

This manual is organized as such to break down some important points about marriage into easy to digest pieces. The divorce rate in the US is hovering around 60% these days. Would you buy a DVD player if you knew that it was 60% likely to fail before it's time? Maybe you would if you knew you could live longer and happier by reading the instructions and properly maintaining it.

Like any product we buy these days, the point of origin is listed somewhere on the box, i.e. "Made in the USA". A wise guy (say, in the presence of women) would say that a marriage would then be "Made in Heaven." Your marriage may have been made in heaven, but it most certainly must be maintained on the ground. To make a marriage wonderful, all the hard work must be performed by you right here on earth.

A wise man and teacher once explained that he was not as brilliant and all-knowing as his students thought. He had just traveled before down the same road that his students were on now. He had fallen in some holes, so now he could warn his students where they were so they wouldn't fall in, too…

I have fallen in many holes. The redeeming advantage of falling in so many holes is developing proficiency in climbing out of them. This book will share what I have learned on the marital journey. And before you think that I might be all-knowing too, remember that many of the greatest coaches in sports were not very good players. My wife can attest to the fact that I should read this book regularly to ensure that I do my part in making our marriage better.

I am not a psychologist, a marriage counselor, anthropologist or therapist. I am also not a cowboy, a rodeo clown, or a brain surgeon for that matter! I am simply a guy who has made mistakes. Who has watched friends and acquaintances make mistakes. Who has thought a lot about what seems to work and what doesn't.

This manual is not based on clinical research. This book is more like a buddy you would call when you're hitting bumps in your marriage, with whom you'd meet over beers to hash things out. Sometimes what you're looking for in that buddy is affirmation of decisions you've already made, other times for answers when you don't have a clue. Sometimes that buddy turns out to be even more confused or screwed up on the topic than you are.

I think (hope) I'm the buddy that has some sound advice. Picture yourself in a bar with that buddy, just hanging out and talking. Have a beer, read this manual, and relax! Maybe this marriage thing doesn't have to be so hard.

Why these instructions are relevant:

Most people don't like to be told what to do. Part of our male stereotype is to be diametrically opposed to asking for directions when lost. While this may be cliché, the fact is that males (married or single) on average die seven years younger than females. Coincidence? As guys, we need to harness our resources if we want to live to our potential.

Your most powerful emotions, talents, skills, or possessions can be your greatest asset and source of comfort and joy, or your greatest liability, even a living nightmare. So it is with marriage. We hope it will be an earthly paradise, but sometimes it can seem like living hell!

Does marriage have to drive you crazy, or worse yet, drive you to an early grave? Is death the only way some of us can get out of our miserable marriages?

Maybe we have no native talent at being husbands and that's why we stink at it. It may not be entirely our fault. After all, how can we be expected to control and master our manly innate animal soul, our strong drive to rule the pride and all of its members? We may be driven to conquer more women and exert more power, but intuitively we know we must tame these urges just to be civilized and certainly to be married.

For better or more likely worse, the male of our species has the reputation of being the more transient of the sexes. We could chalk it up to cavewomen having been less mobile, consumed with caring for infants while the cavemen went out to club an animal on the head. We could also blame our behavior on the magical Y chromosome and its manly side effects. We could even blame

Hollywood because it features a parade of beautiful-beyond-reality females who make us think we could someday get to know perhaps one of them.

Why does any man really want to be married? The fact is marriage is hard work. Then again, being single and social is also hard work. In fact, being single and NOT social (in quiet desperation) is probably the easiest lifestyle to have, if it just weren't so LONELY.

Any married man, especially one with children, can appreciate moments of quiet. Whether the wife is away on a girl's weekend or she is at her parents with the kids, these moments of self-indulgence are sometimes worth coveting. The notion of reading the paper, watching sports, playing golf, etc., without feelings of guilt or animosity is priceless. Quiet isn't a problem until it comes in large doses. Then it's called loneliness. Marriage eliminates the loneliness factor by providing us with a lifelong companion.

Marriage is work because it is a voluntary surrender of autonomy. The formidable "I" has to become "we". The "I want" has to transform itself into "we want". In other words, how you perceive the situation has to change.

At weddings, we get to hear the rhetoric of "two becoming one." You may have seen people join two lit candle flames as a visual symbol of their new bond. The problem with flame as a metaphor is that it can spread wildly unless carefully contained. The flame can only burn for the length of the wick. Wax can build up around it prematurely and snuff it out (divorce). Other candles can be lit from it too and no one would ever know from looking (infidelity). A big cow could kick you in the marriage and burn down Chicago. (SCARY!) Fire warms us, light us and cooks our food, yet it also can burn, scorch and consume. As I said: a tremendous force that can be a great asset or a dangerous liability.

I digress. Again, the question is, "Why would any guy want to get married?" There are right answers and many wrong ones. One excellent reason to stay married was attributed to Robin Williams: "Divorce for a man is the process of having his genitals ripped out through his wallet."

QUICK SETUP

If you are anything like me, you probably don't read manuals. Maybe you are more proud of the notion that you can figure out complex projects without the hand-holding of instructions. Maybe you are too impatient to slow down and walk through the information in a gradual manner. Maybe you are plain lazy! Me? I've been all three over the years, but those are some of the aforementioned "holes" I've created for myself.

Some of you can't help yourselves and have skipped right to this section anyway. If you want to know how to get married in "Quick Setup" mode, here's what you need to do:

Find a girl and marry her.

It's that simple. Actually, it's not that simple. I find that when I approach important tasks with a "Quick Setup" mentality, I next have to go directly to the "Troubleshooting" section to figure out why things aren't working. Whether you are assembling a bookshelf or program-ming a video recorder, some things require a measure of preparation and thought.

> "Marriage has many pains, but celibacy has no pleasures."
>
> *Samuel Johnson*

If you just can't wait to work diligently through this material and give it your undivided 60 minutes, I'll throw you a bone of hard-earned info:

If you want to live the good life, make your wife number one, even above the children. She comes first! It might be easy for either one or both of you to make your career or your children number one, but it's a mistake. A wife that becomes a full time taxi service for the children is making her marriage part-time. Dedicating all your time to raising the kids consumes all of your energy, leaving nothing for your precious marriage. You will lose the bond and intimacy that can only be maintained with the regular nourishment of a quantity of time together. Suddenly, when the kids are grown or independent, you will face a huge loss: you no longer know your spouse. You grew apart as you went in different directions, blinded by the demands of raising children. You see too late that you were separated in all but name, and that it is now almost impossible to instantly renew your relationship .

Make time for your wife daily. Some couples with children carve out 10-15 minutes of private spousal time together prior to dinner. It is at least as important to have quantity time as it is to have quality time. Quantity and frequency are paramount. The daily time together does not require meaningful planning and heavy conversation. In fact, time together must involve non-business-partner-type conversation.

Forget that you two are the CEOs, founders, presidents, and chief operating officers of the family. Find some time to just hang out like you did during courtship. You must strike a balance between running the family and enjoying the company of your spouse simply for the pleasure of each other's presence. It is healthy for your children to realize that Mom and Dad have a "thing" together. Hopefully, the kids will model after the two of you and have great marriages too.

Time with your wife is indispensable to maintaining a meaningful marriage. If you are employed, especially self-employed, compare the hours you spend regularly with your colleagues to the amount of time you spend with your spouse.

An obvious danger: do you spend more time with the women you work with than your wife? Have you noticed how many doctors are married to nurses?

PARTS AND ASSEMBLY

No owner's manual is complete without a list of parts included (usually no batteries!) As guys, we are accustomed to diagrams and packages of nuts and bolts. Marriage doesn't have such concrete ingredients, but I propose that certain pieces of our anatomy come into play in the relationship arena.

There are three principal male body parts involved in selecting a mate. These are the **Heart**, the **Head** and (to gratuitously use an "H" word) the **Hamhock**. In short, these parts represent emotion, rational thought, and sexuality.

The **Heart** is doubtless the noblest part to use in decision-making. This is the part that joins the two of you for no other reason than you are absolutely in love with your best friend. Chicks dig this reason. Meg Ryan has built a successful career in movies based on this body part. I recommend that you mention only this body part when publicly discussing your future with her and others of her kind.

> waponi chief: "Do you want to marry him?"
>
> patricia: "Yes."
>
> waponi chief: "Do you want to marry her?"
>
> joe banks: "Yes."
>
> waponi chief: "Good. You're married."
>
> *Joe Versus the Volcano*
> *Samuel Johnson*

The **Head** is more practical. It brings up the issues of financial and social stability. It asks the question, "Am I upgrading my social status with this merger?" It also takes into consideration whether family and friends like your potential mate. Compatibility of religion and work schedules also comes into play. The head is involved if you are considering marriage to be a "smart move".

Finally, we come to the **Hamhock**. The Weenie. The Willy. The John Thomas, the Dick, the Ding-Dong, the Love Missile, the Trouser Snake, the Short Sword, the Little Head. For better or worse, the Hamhock comes into play more often in mate selection than it probably should. Of the three, this male body part is the one that looks at HER body parts. This part tells you that you are in love based on what she does specifically for IT. This is also the part that can get you into big trouble. Think Vegas weddings. Think shotgun weddings.

I hope that you follow the input of all three parts while seeking a spouse. If a woman has the qualities that appeal to all three, I say "Hold on to that one!" Two out of three isn't bad in many situations, but marriage is too important to get sloppy with details. For example, if you are crazy about an incredibly hot (Hamhock –check!) woman who is perfect for you (Heart –check!) but happens to be already married to your best friend, use your Head and look elsewhere. Let me go one step further:

Beware of the Hamhock:

What if your main consideration was lust, i.e., Mr. Hamhock? Lust for a spouse is certainly appropriate and desirable. The physical relationship is one of the foundations of a solid marriage. However, once you make the leap into marriage, it is no longer desirable or even safe to follow your Hamhock. Your Hamhock is powerful but not very discriminate. It may continue tempting you to appreciate the beauty of other women and draw you to them.

The animal drive that is present in almost all people has the ability to trick the brain into believing that following Mr. Hamhock is okay. It is not okay, because it can lead you into bigger trouble than your brain can rescue you from. After you are married we urge you to put your head in command with your heart following as directed; Hamhock satisfaction will naturally ensue.

To control your animal inclination, develop your head's innate ability to guide your behavior into thoughtful actions. Your task as a husband can be defined in five simple functions:

> to express words of loving kindness,
>
> to listen to her,

to perform countless actions of loving kindness,

to express gratitude, and

to display affection.

As long as your head and heart keep you focused on those five roles and responsibilities of a husband, you stay out of the doghouse, in the main house, with abundant time in the cradle of love to satisfy your Hamhock's desires.

Note: If you've found "THE ONE"…

You followed my advice and have found someone who meets all three body-part criteria. You've found your soul mate, your one and only, your eternal love.

CONGRATULATIONS! You know she is THE ONE because of your common interests, her humor, her intelligence, her volunteer work, her way with kids, and some other attributes. Odds are, you're not so much wrong as optimistic. Destiny brought you together. You beat the odds. Of the four billion people on this planet, you somehow stumbled onto the one, solitary, single female whose puzzle piece matches yours.

> "The female woman is one of the greatest institooshuns of which this land can boste."
>
> *Artemus Ward*

Get real! Don't be offended, though. If you believe what you say, more power to you. Your attitude is your strength. You are obviously optimistic and will to try to see things through. But bear with me while I tell you why I suggest that we all consider that we've found "A ONE" instead of "THE ONE". Why not recognize the fact that there are many people out there in this world with whom you could foster a fantastic, life-fulfilling relationship? The key to marriage is not your luck in the draw, but your willingness to make things work.

Any one who is out there still looking for "THE ONE" should change his approach. If you look for "A ONE," then the scope of the search is realistically altered to reduce the stress of the journey. Finding "THE ONE" would be an arduous task that could stretch on for years or decades. Even after marriage, you would still be tempted each time you'd meet someone to think that she could truly be the "THE ONE." And so, in fact, your current spouse would only be "THE ONE" until you discovered "THE EVEN BETTER ONE".

Unfortunately, interviewing more potential spouses will not reduce the number of remaining applicants. It will more likely create narrower criteria as your cravings for perfection are indulged, honed and fine-tuned. Guess what?

You're still getting older at the same time! This is reducing your own value as a potential mate and could leave you an unchosen chooser. Look hard and look as long as you must, but be conscious not to over-look. No one person will ever have the ability to meet all of your expectations. Likewise, you will never be able to meet every desire of your future wife. All humans make mistakes and have their foibles. After all, we are only human.

Even if you live with her before marriage, you will not truly know her as if you were married. In fact, the higher divorce rates of those who don't delay cohabitation until after marriage indicates that there might be some harm in living together first.

Marriage is very different than living together prior to marriage. One becomes accustomed to the concept of living together with the safety net of having the ability to break up if better opportunities present. Living with one foot out of the door already, it's so

much easier to bail when things don't go right. And a faulty premise will lead to a wrong conclusion: "She's changed, I'm outta here!"

We can't expect perfection on a platter. A few important criteria though will help us focus in on someone whom we could dedicate ourselves to in a marriage that would stand a chance. On my short-list of solid, workable criteria: kindness, trust, integrity, parenting ability, similar values, and high level of sexual attraction. Aren't these the kinds of basic qualities one would reasonably and objectively look for in a potential mate?

If you're reading this book and have found that potential mate, think of her as "A ONE" and love her as "THE ONE" until the day you die. Then you are a winner. In fact, if you think of her as "A-1" (as in A-OK, not the sauce), then your attitude is adjusted perfectly. There will always be other women encountered in your life who are smarter, prettier, friendlier, etc, etc, and sometimes all of these at once. That's where you have to realize that these women are just others in the "A ONE" category… and go home! Consider these women as "A-1" women just like your wife. They are not competitors but colleagues.

Other body parts for consideration….

Another body part that bears recognition in the mating process is the eye. Of course, the eyes are important in establishing a first impression and perceiving a possible love "at first sight". On a deeper level, the eyes are more than just a sensory organ for visible attributes, but for all aspects of a person. This baits the adage, "Is true love blind to the faults of the beloved?"

Love is not blind. As a matter of fact, you will find that shortly after the last piece of wedding cake is eaten, your wife's weak points will become more sharply visible. For some, the painstaking process of watching your future spouse consult and deliberate for days, weeks and months about the wedding itself is an indication. The multitude of advisors, planners, and interested family members called in over the monumental decision of whether to use egg-white or whipped-cream icing or white- or buff-colored envelopes for the response cards to your wedding invitation could provide a clue that she may not meet your definition of perfect in every way.

Besides, it's important to realize that while she is being assessed and judged during the wedding-planning process, she, in turn, is internalizing your role and learning some things about you. Are you pitching in, indulgent, compulsive, passive-aggressive, impatient, controlling, enthusiastic, supportive, etc.? Although she may seem distracted by seemingly endless and ridiculous details, you can be sure that she's taking it all in to be analyzed and mulled over later.

Consider that, for many of us, those that have loved us longest —our parents and possibly siblings —are typically our most prolific critics. Love isn't blind; it is more of a magnifying glass. Try to focus on the positive. Open your eyes to her attributes, and close them to her flaws.

She is probably not perfect, but then, you certainly are not perfect either. You can't be! You are one of us, a "he".

Given our less-than-saintly status, it must not be such an easy task to love, cherish, and support us during the good and the bad

> "I'll be the first to admit that it's possible that you did marry the wrong person. However, if you treat the wrong person like the right person, you could well end up having married the right person after all."
>
> *Zig Ziglar*

times. If she were perfect, it would be easy for her to be so good to us. She may realize that she is not perfect and perhaps spends energy trying to overcome her challenges and shortcomings. The fact that she has the energy and presence to overcome her weaknesses and still be a caring and loving wife makes her all the more remarkable.

Her imperfections are all the more reason to love and appreciate her. And the best we can hope for is that she return the favor.

In keeping with the "parts list" mentality, we have reviewed some of the parts to consider in a spouse. Just as important, we should consider our own parts as well.

Do you have parts missing?

What guy hasn't seen the movie, "Rocky"? Rocky Balboa is a brutish, inarticulate, meat-punching boxer who happens to be in love. He is also a classic movie hero. Although his elocution left something to be desired, Rocky was brilliant when he talked about his marriage with Adrienne. When Rocky was asked why he wanted to marry the quiet and gentle Adrienne, he said "Because together we fill gaps."

Rocky was right. You should marry your spouse for things other than her resume. If you are trying to marry up by finding someone of wealth with impressive parents and ancestors, a high level of education, uncommon beauty, great athletic prowess, or a great job, you may be deeply disappointed down the road.

There is a dangerous hazard lurking when a marriage is founded by the urge to marry up. Things can go wrong with careers, wealth, and possessions, and beauty and athletic ability can fade. If that is the basis of your marriage, what's left? More than the possessions that you obtain, the trips that you take, the cars that you own, and your success together in the husband-wife putt-putt league, you will truly need your spouse to be with you during your times of crisis, misery, bankruptcy, illness, injury, and before you die.

Rocky was right that you need your spouse to fill gaps. This means that you are not perfect. (Tough idea, but it should sound familiar by now.) In fact, you have some missing parts that the right spouse can supply to make a whole. So don't expect your spouse to be perfect. Accept her deficiencies as you expect her to accept yours. If you become more proficient at being a spousal critic, you will become a miserable person for your spouse to live with.

A very bright teacher once explained to me that in many languages the word for "I" is written with lower-case letters. In America, though, we always capitalize "I" when we write. This is clear reflection of our cultural tendency to focus on our singular personal needs. In a marriage the focus really needs to be on what you can do for your spouse, not what she can do for you.

OPERATION

Now is the time where a manual is supposed to tell you to hit the ON button and smoothly operate your product. Since we aren't dealing with an actual product, this section is modified to address some of the vast components of man/woman interaction.

We know that men and women are different. Some guys may have some feminine qualities and vice-versa, but when it comes right down to it, we pretty much are destined to think and react differently based on our gender. What matters is tolerance of these differences. As Rodney King once put it: "Why can't we all just get along?"

I would love to be able to tell you that your love for each other is all you need to conquer the obstacles that come through life and marriage. Love by itself will not conquer all that much, really. It will be your commitment, deeds, actions and your behavior that will do all the conquering in your relationship with your wife and others. You need the actions and good deeds to take place on a daily basis.

> "People are often enamored with my Super Bowl ring. But it's my wedding ring that I'm most proud of. And having a good marriage takes even more work than winning a Super Bowl."
>
> *Trent Dilfer*
> *Seattle Seahawks quarterback*

Consider the effort to maintaining the quality of your marriage as analogous to pushing a boulder up the mountain. As long as you keep working at pushing the boulder up, your relationship will get stronger. When the effort is missing, the boulder does not just stop going up the mountain—it starts to roll back down.

Complacency in your marriage or your business won't stop change; it will just make sure that you won't be controlling it. Things get better or worse; rarely do they remain static. Complacency typically results in regression. Keep up the daily effort to nurture the relationship.

Understanding the opposite sex.

You may have heard that you must understand your wife in order to have a good marriage. Wrong. It probably cannot be done, at least not in the first decades of a marriage. Understanding will certainly not be gleaned by living together before marriage, nor is understanding your spouse even essential. Instead of wasting energy and promoting premature male pattern baldness while you search for understanding, focus on a cause of paramount importance: commitment.

Commitment is the glue that holds a marriage together. Marriage is not based on understanding each other, but on commitment to each other. It is not necessary to understand each of your wife's idiosyncrasies to have a level of commitment necessary for bonding you together in marital bliss.

For example, let's turn our attention to her lifestyle choices.

The purpose behind buying the glass trinkets neatly stacked in the dining room buffet is not important. Nor is the reason for picking up all the valuable items at the flea market. And do not try to penetrate the mystery as to why it is

nearly impossible for some women to pass within three miles of a shoe store without visiting and trying on two or three dozen shoes.

Perhaps, you think, it makes sense for men to enroll their wives in the shoe-of-the-month club. Have the new shoe model sent to your wife each and every month in her favorite colors. It may cost less, you say, to buy all the extra shoes than to have her spend countless hours, days, weeks or years over a lifetime trying on all the shoes at every available opportunity.

Sounds logical, but don't sign up. It's possible that she simply requires the time away from us. Maybe the game of trying on every shoe in every shoe store is a good relief from the domestic burden she feels at home despite our dedicated effort to help around the house during commercials and halftime. It may even be that shopping makes more sense than the hours we spend watching reruns of ball games that took place 12 years ago on ESPN Classics. It should be universally accepted that we feel compelled to watch the Ali-Frazier-Foreman fights from the 70's and

> "I didn't marry you because you were perfect. I didn't even marry you because I loved you. I married you because you gave me a promise."
>
> *Thornton Wilder*
> *The Skin of Our Teeth*

80's on an annual basis—but regrettably, she cannot understand this. Just so, we cannot understand her requirement to shop. Don't even try.

Your understanding of the "why" behind her behavior will not in any way make you love her more or make you a better husband. Why she requires 90 minutes in the bathroom before leaving the house should make no difference to you. Stick to your job description. Your devotion is total; therefore, it is not important to try to understand. Analyzing the situation will be adding gas to the flames of bewilderment. Capitulate! She is hard-wired the way she is and will not and does not want to change. You cannot understand her because she is a woman. It may be that after many decades of marriage, you will at last attain understanding and clarity. It may also be that you will simply lose the compulsion to know the why.

Now that you understand that you do not need to understand your wife, let's talk commitment. As part of the yoke of commitment, consider and consistently demonstrate your total devotion to her. Support her in all her endeavors. Do not make the mistake of saying that this or that is her gig and she is on her own with those parts of her life. Get behind her and be committed as long as her interests are legal and moral.

Rolling your eyes and negative body language when discussing her activities and interests is a sign of weakness and of a flimsy level of devotion. Stand by your woman. Support her when she complains how unfair her boss is for making her waste time by completing expense reports after a work related trip. Agree with her that the boss is an unjust tyrant that should be fired and then placed in a public stockade. Your commitment empowers you to listen to her despite your lack of interest or utter boredom. Paying attention to her views and thoughts gives her renewed vitality.

Total devotion means sticking behind your spouse, protecting her, giving her honor, and stroking her ego. Intuitively, you know not to encourage or allow disparaging remarks about your wife to be said around you. In fact, make it your intent to never even compromise the marital relations of any couple. For example, avoid bad mouthing another guy's wife even if he is trying to get you to voice a scathing opinion about her. If you encourage a friend to be critical of his spouse, you may then open the door for him to do the same to you. Besides the terrible crime of compromising a friend's marriage, you may be making your own marriage vulnerable to attack.

I know a guy who was talking with a buddy in a bar about marriage issues (just like we are right now!). The friend was feeling down because he just separated from his wife and was looking for support. My friend thought he was helping out by honestly stating all the things that were wrong about this woman so he would see that he was better off without her. Makes sense.

That is, until the couple got back together in the end! That's a relationship that will be awkward for a long time! Take my advice and just don't even go there. Be a friend, but throwing out bad vibes about others usually ends up coming back around in an unpleasant way.

Maturity levels between the sexes.

So, your wife says that you are immature. She may be correct. To be qualified for marriage, a man hopefully will have gained a thorough understanding of himself. After a youth of developing a strong ego, he can appreciate what it is to have the flames of the ego stoked. It's an overwhelming gratification. It's also addictive.

When a man finally understands that an ego trip is a trip to nowhere he may be ready for marriage. The only redeeming aspect of building your own ego is to serve as training to care for the egos of those you care about. When you can use your intimate knowledge of nurturing, feeding, and enriching an ego to give to your loved one a sense of being appreciated, then you are a big enough man to make a great marriage.

When you have mastered your craving to be honored and can direct your focus on honoring your woman, you may be ready for marriage. When you can stop trying to force the world to respect you and focus instead on respecting your woman, you may be ready for marriage.

Have you stopped needing appreciation, respect, admiration, and honor from every co-worker at the office, from every neighbor on the block, and from everyone else you may happen to meet? Good! Use the knowledge gained in your earlier pursuit of honor to guide you in giving appreciation, honor, admiration, respect and regular broad stroking to the ego of your woman. Now you know how to make a wonderful marriage.

 Dedicate your cravings to her. Overindulge her! She is likely more skilled at controlling hedonistic tendencies than you are. It is okay and even desirable for you to fire your ego—or at least, demote it. Life becomes much easier and less painful. A most wonderful side effect of downsizing your ego is that you get rid of a lot of pain. And think of all the energy you have at your marriage's disposal when you are not consumed with cultivating and protecting your own ego.

> "Marriage is our last, best chance to grow up."
>
> *Joseph Barth*

You may get the notion that now that you are married, anything goes in the house. After all, she is your wife. I suggest that you maintain a certain special level of decorum when you are in the presence of your wife. Your relationship with her is special and unique. Regardless of how close you are and how long you have been married, the singular specialness with her cannot be the same if you use your "locker room" vocabulary when she is within earshot.

I know that you are very proud of the accomplishment of being able to burp the entire alphabet in two breaths. Your buddies would be proud of you for that.

But not your wife.

Her ears do not appreciate that kind of music, or the music from the more southerly opening. As a matter of fact, the "dutch oven" (where you flatulate under the bedcovers and put her head under there with the malodorous biscuit) is a hilarious gag, but don't do it. Your buddies will love to hear about it, but you may be sleeping on the couch for a month.

Consider your bathroom activities. She really is pleased that you took some initiative regarding personal hygiene, but becomes disturbed upon finding your toothpaste and spittle remnants mixed with shaven whisker stubble and trimmed nose hairs in your shared bathroom sink. The presence of the aforementioned bodily detritus need not be displayed in the sink as evidence that you exercised personal hygiene to her specifications. Your cleanliness will suffice as proof.

It is not important for you to try and figure out why she finds it upsetting that you leave a potpourri of trimmed-away parts in your bathroom. All you need to know is that the discovery is always going to upset her and you should avoid that by the adding the step of rinsing the bowl. The rinsing procedure may take an additional 30 seconds out of your already packed schedule, but it is worth the Herculean effort involved.

Equally difficult (due to the enormous amount of lifting required) is the toilet seat. Granted, someone has to change the position of the seat after you drain the lizard, take a squirt, and break the seal. Reasonable men might conclude that alternating the arduous task of moving the seat with the other family members that use the commode would be a fair solution and would help preserve the health of your sorely overworked back. But it isn't always about being reasonable. Yes, I know that even the mere thought of raising and lowering the seat causes that sore lumbar disk to bulge. No matter— raise and lower the seat! Let's steal a slogan here and say, "Just do it"! Lift the seat before you void and lower the seat after the last shake every time you urinate indoors.

Why should you do it every time? Why, because, it's part of your job description as a husband. I know of a friend who simply takes a seat every time he uses the bathroom at home. No mess is created and the seat is always down.

This next statement may be shocking to you, but you must trust me on this one. Resist the temptation of showing your wife the fantastic movement you placed in the toilet. Regardless of the magnitude, shape, or aroma of your effort, do not show it to her or even brag about it. Flush twice or three times if necessary to eliminate every trace of the prize-winning bowel evacua-

tion. A lighted match or two will do wonders to minimize permanent damage to her olfactory bulb, and her sexual desire for you. Don't do anything to lower that. Lower the seat instead!

The extra seconds of labor you invest in the bathroom are precious to her, and in some cases to any human that requires the use of a bathroom after your invasion. Why your wife wouldn't be proud of the spectacle in the toilet, I don't know. I don't understand women completely; remember, I am a man. But I can assure you that I am correct.

Your willingness to observe a higher level of decorum includes giving her privacy in the bathroom and the bedroom. When your young children are in the bathroom, the door is open and you walk in and out. Don't treat your wife like a young child. She must feel she has a special position and role in the house.

Even with privacy, she and her body remain dedicated and loyal to you; it's just that her body is not available for your inspection and pleasure at all times. There is nothing special about something that is at your beck and call 24/7/365. If she occasionally brushes off your attempts at romantic advances, avoid the temptation of questioning her commitment to you. After all, she already demonstrated her devotion to you—she married you with all your idiosyncrasies and flaws. She may have even worked with you in creating children that may be a bit like you! She can remain devoted to you, caring, loving, and interested in you without having to perform in the sack, in the car, on the table, or in your favorite corner each and every day at the very moment you feel moved.

> sam baldwin: "Well I'm not looking for a mail-order bride! I just want somebody I can have a decent conversation with over dinner. Without it falling down into weepy tears over some movie!"
>
> greg: "She's, as you just saw, very emotional."
>
> sam baldwin: "Although I cried at the end of 'the dirty dozen.'"
>
> greg: "Who didn't?"
>
> *sleepless in seattle*

Ladies and Gentlemen...

If you are seeing that showing tact and maturity are crucial to this marriage thing, you are getting the point. You used to open doors for her. You had the superhuman power to wait until she started eating before you devoured your meal. You scraped her icy windows before she left the house. You insisted on carrying her luggage and heavy trash despite your recently herniated lumbar disks. You frequently acknowledged her beauty and how lucky you were to have her. You demonstrated incredible restraint and used only appropriate language around her. You actually put the newspaper down to listen to her.

You even may have looked at her when there was not a commercial break on the TV. Maybe you had the ability to resist the temptation to ask her to hold her thought until the weather forecast was finished on the TV news. Your rekindled efforts will be meaningful to her, fulfilling to you, and foster further kindness towards each other.

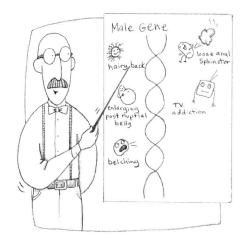

Kindness can start off an upward spiral of further kind acts. The more nice things you say and do for her, the more nice things she will say and do for you. Regrettably, the downward spiral can be faster. Mean-spirited words and acts will certainly produce more of the same from her. Translation: you probably won't get lucky that night.

The wedding ring may be a circle without end, but as you try to climb the marital mountain, you want to ascend as well as go around. Think of an upward spiral. Your marriage can be an upward-spiraling coil stretched all the way to the heavens.

You are in a challenging endeavor; maintaining a powerful love with your spouse is a continuous battle against the odds. People we grew up loving were our blood relatives: parents, grandparents, and siblings. But remember, your wife is not allowed to be family member prior to marriage (in most states of the Union). Loving her, a non-family member, day and night is challenging and will not come naturally.

She probably has the same feelings about you, especially if she grew up without any brothers. She may not initially realize that men are the way we are, that many of our undesirable attributes are innate phenomena. It may be that when you help her make a son she can better appreciate you because will see that many of these inherent traits are present from birth. She may even appreciate that you have overcome many of these undesirable characteristics, with the determined and unrelenting help of your mother.

If you want to be treated like a king, you'll need to coronate a Queen. Remind your queen of her royal status and treat her like a queen on a daily basis; she'll make sure you become a king. And a king who wishes to remain always happy and gratified will perpetuate the courtship with

becky: "Verbal ability is a highly overrated thing in a guy, and it's our pathetic need for it that gets us into so much trouble."

sleepless in seattle

his queen.

Let's Talk —the value of Communication:

How could lack of communication be an issue in our modern society? We have so many tools of communication: fax, e-mail, voice mail, cordless phones, text messaging, mobile phones, pagers, instant messaging, e-mail in our phones, banners from small airplanes… Why is lack of communication the apparent culprit in many marriages?

In part, it's because we reserve the use of the aforementioned communication tools exclusively for business or for keeping up with our buddies on the scores and the Vegas odds on the upcoming games.

Why not use some of these tools for sending romantic messages to your wife? Who knows, you might get lucky over your lunch break. It's a great feeling to know that when our pager rings, it is not always bad news from the office. It may be your wife trying to respond to a hot message requesting immediate emergency attention at the home, a hotel, or a secluded place near your office.

We don't hesitate to spend a few extra bucks on lawn fertilizer to ensure the health of our lawns. Thirty or even one hundred dollars for a spontaneous lunchtime rendezvous with your spouse is an inexpensive outlay with a guaranteed excellent return on your investment.

Find ways to make good use of those high-tech means of communicating. When communicating, consider the messages that you leave. Are they all a giant "honey-do" list? Are your conversations more like business partners discussing the ongoing business of running a household full of children and all the attendant responsibilities? Are the remarks primarily argumentative or critical?

If you want to come home to a receptive and eager-to-see-you spouse, make sure that you leave messages and notes that are not just demands or to-do lists. Think of complimentary, romantic, and affectionate remarks too. You want to tip the positive-to-negative ratio in favor of her feeling good about her and you!

Don't forget your griping-to-thanking ratio either. When we don't get what we want or are not happy with spousal behavior, we tend to criticize in hyperbole and with a raised voice. The entire county hears us gripe when we are unhappy with such major infractions as buying the wrong brand of beer for the upcoming poker night or turning on the vacuum and/or garbage disposal during a ball game. On the other hand, when our needs are met, we whisper and mumble "thank you"— if we remember at all.

The time and energy required to express your gratitude is measured in seconds. Make it a habit.

The three most important words:

While we are talking about communication, we must review three crucial words to live by in a happy marriage. You may immediately assert that these words would be "I love you," and you would be right if it were the three words you should SAY to your wife with meaning. I counter that there are three more words that you should LIVE BY to be happy…

The first word of the three is simply "Sorry." When you screw up, and you are being defensive and argumentative, there is often a particle of truth in the accusation. Genuinely expressing sorrow, you too can add or restore peace to your home. We all know of parents and kids that don't speak, or siblings that are on bad terms….How many broken family relationships could be salvaged if someone was BIG enough to say, sorry.

The other two words go together, and they are simply "So what." When things go wrong, especially when you clearly feel that the situation is not your fault but is due to something your spouse did or didn't do, remember the big picture. Ask yourself:

> Whatever it is that your spouse just did or didn't do that has you upset: Will it matter in 18 minutes, will it matter in 18 weeks?

> Will you even remember it in 18 months or 18 years?

> Is it worth compromising the peace in your home? If not SHUT UP, think SO WHAT! Don't ever miss an opportunity to keep your mouth shut…

Most often the answer to any question of this nature is No. Maybe you can prevent the problems that drive you crazy. A lot of these problems come from unrealistic allocation of marital responsibilities. Great marriages often have couples that specialize in tasks. Maybe you can find an alternate way to deal with your dry cleaning problems, pick up/delivery service, if it's such a priority, do it yourself! Maintaining a clean house with lots of kids is overwhelming.

If it drives you crazy, hire a cleaning crew, teach the kids to clean, or clean yourself!

The business of marriage.

If you know how to be successful in business then you can certainly be successful in marriage. The method: always treat your spouse as well as you treat your best customer or best source of business referrals. When trying to get a customer to buy, there is no limit to how kind, courteous and thoughtful we can be.

Try the same techniques on your wife. We all know how to play customer golf: we allow our customers to win the game. Let your wife win. She will buy!

Other than the above, there is precious little in common between your marriage and your business.

Successful businessmen, watch out. You have already made the marriage deal. Resist the temptation to think of your wife as an acquisition to compare with other men's acquisitions. If you made it big, you cannot think about upgrading wives to match the new you. The wild success that you have had since you married does not entitle you to find a new wife to fit the part.

> "Whenever you're wrong, admit it; whenever you're right, shut up."
>
> *Ogden Nash*

Likewise, don't waste energy trying to make her change with your bank account. She is not an object to be bought. She is your soul mate that enriches your soul. If the situation reversed itself and business declined or became bankrupt, she would still love you unless your soul or character became bankrupt.

She married you for your character, your soul, your devotion to her and her alone, your kindness, and total commitment to her. The fluctuations of the stock market are not connected to the reasons that she loved you.

If you develop a wildly profitable position in your business life, use it to strengthen the relations that mean the most to you. Take advantage of the countless opportunities wealth affords to strengthen your marriage and family ties by loosening the requirements you have to your career, by saving for your retirement, by building the children's college fund, and funding your growing empire.

With the multitude of talents you must have in making your clients and customers buy into you, selling yourself to your wife should be a cinch. After all, she already bought into you: she married you. Put your best tactics to work.

She can recommit and you can fend off any buyer's remorse that she may be experiencing. You have the talent and know-how, and if you have the interest, you will be successful.

Of course, managing a business also entails managing assets. Marriage is similar. (In a divorce, the material ones definitely come to light.) A happy marriage requires harmonious management of assets, both tangible and intangible. The word "love" in Hebrew is "Ahuva". The root of this word "Hav" is translated as "to give." Marriage is all about giving and sharing. Any person who has lived alone for a while can easily get into the groove of a free-time free-fall. A guy can wake up on Saturday morning, look at the ceiling for five minutes, turn on the sports channel for 18 more minutes, roll out of bed and eat half of a grapefruit and then scratch himself and look out the window for three minutes more, all without uttering a sound.

In a marriage, time, a most precious commodity, must be shared. Marriage does not dictate that you get up and spend that exact same time period serving your wife breakfast in bed, but whatever you plan to do that day has to take her expectations into account. If you are lucky, she may want to watch the sports channel with you or perhaps she will want the other half of the grapefruit. Either way, it's not a bad idea to communicate your intentions for the day ahead of time so you can mentally accept that after the grapefruit you are both going to shop for wallpaper.

> "There is nothing more admirable than two people who see eye-to-eye keeping house as man and wife, confounding their enemies, and delighting their friends."
>
> *Homer, 9th century BC*

A major part of this sharing involves another commodity, money. As stated previously, money can be a wonderful adjunct to enriching your marriage. It can release you from the frustrations of the workplace, and you can devote to your family a lot of time and energy that you would have needed otherwise just to get them life's necessities. And of course, money gives your generosity power, allowing you and your family to bring much good to your community and people in need.

However, the pursuit of money can ruin marriages. Some feel that money issues are the number one reason for marital troubles. Oddly enough, it has been found that those people with the most money also have the most worries over money matters! So be wise. If you have money, use it to make your marriage better by making more time for each other and by working together to repair some of the ills of the community.

Women are sometimes seen as sex symbols whereas men are compared as success symbols. In that regard, success is sexy. But money, like sex, will test you: will you own it or will it rule you?

We may be tied to the things we NEED, like food and shelter, but it's the things we WANT that are more likely to lead to problems. When friends, neighbors, or even acquaintances acquire a new car, piece of furniture, jewelry, etc., it is human nature for us to think about acquiring something similar for ourselves. To discuss these issues with any sense of reason, spouses need to have a grasp of how their money is already being spent and the role and purpose of money in their lives. Even if only one of you sits down and pays the bills, both need to know how much is left over for buying the WANTS after the NEEDS have been met.

Thankfully, all that is NEEDED for us to survive is provided in abundance or at minimal cost: including air, water, red eye airline tickets to Vegas, fuel for warmth, food, photos, Sports Illustrated, memories, cable TV, hand-made cards and gifts, the presence of loved ones, and personal notes.

On the other hand, all of those precious items that are only WANTED are relatively scarce or very expensive such as diamonds, bright red European sports cars, rare pieces of art, luxury suites at the stadium with a parking pass, finely crafted furniture and rare collectables.

When people or those they love are ill or near death, they seek and find comfort predominantly in all that was listed as abundant and inexpensive: the NEEDS rather than those expensive WANTS. No one dies regretting the time spent with their loved ones. Why then spend a lifetime accumulating or coveting things that won't matter that much in the end?

Nonmaterial wants and needs.

In the last section, we were talking about stuff. What we want to do and need to do can also be at odds for a happy marriage. Once you know that you want a good marriage it involves doing what you need to do, not what you want or feel like doing.

When your wife is asking you questions or asks you to move something heavy at the wrong time, you feel like watching the TV until a commercial break, you feel like finishing the newspaper, you feel like finishing the chapter in the book before you chat with her because that is what you feel like doing. But you have already decided that what you want is a great marriage. Therefore, stop what you are doing and listen to her, now. That is what she needs and you need to do.

Any objective, whether it is related to your health, your career, learning, and your relationships with parents, children, friends, requires you having the discipline to do what you "need" to do, not always what you "feel" like doing at the moment...

When you force yourself to do what you "need" to do, rather then what you "feel" like doing, you are exercising "free will". Free will is not doing what you feel whenever you feel the desire. That is being enslaved to your desires or animal drive rather than you cognitive wants. That is the big difference between people and critters. We have the discipline to do what we "need" subjugating our desires to do what we "feel". We pursue our objectives rather than scratching ourselves, eating, burping, and sleeping whenever we feel like it.

You want a great marriage, translated; you want and need to give her pleasure, attention, and affection. Remember, the root word of Ahava is to give. Love is an active verb involving continuous giving, nurturing and courting of her.

Sex! Sex! Sex!

I'm sure you were wondering when we would get to this section! In so many ways, women are different from men. They are equal but different. One area of particular difference is that we live for the sexual act. Women also are crazy for the sexual act but they are also deeply interested in the happenings before the act (foreplay) and the happenings after the act. In other words, try to say something complimentary after the climax but before you fall asleep.

Remember back to the early days of the relationship? You were hungry for more and went for it. Try something new and go for a second round of fun and games. Perhaps in the privacy of your bedroom you'd like to experiment with toys or instructive films to stoke your flames. Go for it! If it brings you closer together and is consensual, then consider it marriage-building.

Work hard to restore or add passion to your sex life. Without it, she may end up competing with your buddies for your attention, time, and interest. She will probably lose out to the buddies...

With some luck, your wife may some day understand that men have an incredibly heavy burden they carry around. Men have a powerful animal soul trying to convince them that having more women is better. Additionally, men's drive to satisfy their thirst for having more sex is analogous to drinking salt water when dehydrated. The more men drink for their sexual appetite, the more thirsty they become. The more women a single man has, the more women that man wants.

A woman should understand that she can and does successfully satisfy her husband but only for the moment or the evening. He will want more very soon. Men need to appreciate that a woman is desirous of sex in a powerful way, maybe even more so than a man, BUT she may be physically exhausted from caring for her man and the children. Remember guys: you did not marry a servant and no concubines allowed.

On this topic, you may find yourself tempted to compare your wife with other women. It could be a comparison to your first wife, previous girlfriend, or any other person you were romantically involved with.

Bad idea.

Being coaxed into lengthy discussions about your premarital or previous marital relations can set you way back. Better to respond to any inquiries by stating that things didn't work out because you were not soul mates. The underlying message behind your willingness to discuss past relationships is that those women are still on your mind.

You truly want to avoid setting up a competition between your wife and the memories of your previous relationships. Regardless of the flattery in which you encase your remarks, they will likely create a negative reaction. Even going down the path of bad-mouthing the others will lead to trouble. Eliminate any thoughts of bringing the topic up and redirect the conversation to other areas.

> "Women need a reason for having sex, men just need a place."
>
> *City Slickers*

Likewise, you are better off not probing into her previous relationships. Curiosity kills the cat. You might not like the answers that she gives nor is it healthy for you to obsess on the behavior of the men she was married to or dated.

Marriage does not mean that the fun of courtship should end. The notion of "Why keep chasing the bus if I've already caught it?" cannot be good for your relationship. The dating becomes more important after the nuptials than before. While dating you can decide that you have the wrong person and begin searching again. Once you are married, you are locked in. You'd best work to make it good.

Have you had the sad occasion to know any close friends who went through a divorce or the death of a spouse? If so, you may have noticed a trend. Single adults seeking companionship tend to return to their "dating weight." While searching for and establishing courtship, the tendency is to obtain a high level of fitness at a body weight that makes one most appealing to the opposite sex.

Don't our spouses deserve some level of effort from us to maintain a reasonable level of physical attractiveness? Obsession at maintaining our "dating weight" is superficial; no one is the same at fifty as he was at twenty. But fortunately, spending years together growing the marriage results in a heightened level of love, which more than offsets our physical failings. Your looks call to mind the ever-growing stack of memories built together, the wonderful time spent with each other, and the physical attraction is more than maintained even as the body ages.

Without obsessing, do your best to maintain some level of fitness for your own health and ability to perform with your mate; at least make the effort to remain attractive. After all, your intimate relations allow you to connect in the deepest, most meaningful emotional way, in a way that only spouses can. It's part of your job to try to remember how creative you were on your dates to make yourself exciting. Remembering how to date, using creativity to be fun and attractive, should lead to exciting sex.

Think back to how hard you were willing to work at courting your spouse. Better yet, think back to how what great lengths you would go to have sexual relations with a female when you first discovered what effect testosterone could have on your brains.

With regard to brains, it has been well documented that man was created with many organs, among them the brain and the penis. Regrettably, man was only given enough blood to operate one of those organs at a time, thereby resulting in our famous foolishness when the blood flows predominately to the lower organ.

While courting my beloved, I personally drove over two hours after a long day of work to be with her, and then returned home just in time to go to work the next morning. Facing the results of sleep deprivation, I knew that my blood supply had definitely NOT been channeling to the organ ABOVE my neck!

Unfortunately, once your woman caves in and shares her body, you may never work as hard to romance her. In fact, many of us consider the act of proposing to our future spouses as our version of "caving in." Singer Meatloaf eloquently portrayed this notion in "Paradise By The Dashboard Light" in which every time his date tries to get a long-term commitment during their passionate encounter, he can only reply with, "Let me sleep on it."

> chelsea: "I really like this guy. I think that Seth could be the one."
>
> holly: "Are you serious? Does he feel the same way?"
>
> chelsea: "Please, he's a man. He has no idea how he's feeling."
>
> *Love stinks*

Long-term gratification in your marriage depends on keeping the courtship going after the wedding bells stop ringing. With time, your ability and creativity in being romantic, passionate and thoughtful in pursuing your wife will pay off in kindness and affection returned. The more you give, the more you get.

A passionate sexual relationship is paramount in a healthy and happy marriage. The pursuit of common interests is greatly overemphasized by the experts. Your buddies probably have many more areas of interest in common with you than your spouse. If you are into following professional sports, playing on a softball team, playing fantasy football, captaining the bowling league, and hosting the monthly poker games, you should have no trouble connecting with your man-friends to hang out. In fact, the time with other guys pursing those interests is desirable and healthy in your marriage.

However, only your spouse can have passionate sex with you. Sorry frat buddies, she wins every time at that. The commonality and intimacy shared with your spouse in the privacy of your bedroom (or private venue of your choice) makes you closer than guessing together which team might be able to put the Yankees down. The bottom line is that manly guys do not have to find their effeminate side to be able to connect with their spouse. Forget it. We don't have to have a feminine side. That theory went out in the 90's. What brings you together is your manliness and her womanliness; that's how you connect.

Your sex life is critical to the health of your marriage. Unhappy couples complain of lost interest in each other. Translation: the sex life has diminished greatly or is nonexistent.

I propose that you do your best to avoid a series of ups and downs in your sex life as it relates to the progression of your relationship. When it comes to the "peaks and valleys" of a marital sex life, living on the mountaintop is certainly appealing. Unfortunately, the chances are good that this great situation cannot be maintained for long. (You are right next to a valley, after all.) Try to live on a "high plateau", instead.

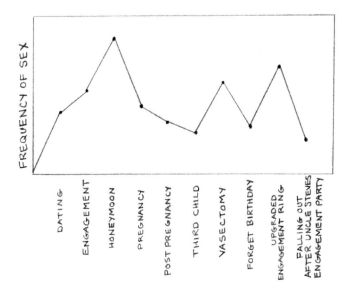

You complain that she forgets to pick up the laundry, or neglects to have your favorite foods in the fridge? I'll bet you wouldn't be complaining about that if your sex life was great.

The first time you were ready to share your bodies together, were you wondering if the laundry was tended to and the fridge properly stocked? Did any of that stuff really matter at the time your desire was building as you began touching? Of course not! You were in hot pursuit. Without a sex life together, the inadequacies of each other become greatly magnified. Guys that were boy scouts, remember how you created that inferno of a campfire? First, you collected kindling and started the fire with a tiny spark, fanned the nearly imperceptible fire, added a bit more wood, more fanning, adding progressively more wood and larger pieces of wood until you had created the huge, roaring, intensely hot, almost out of control fire. That is how you rebuild the sexual fire from the spark that is ever present in your wife. She has the desire, ability, and pilot light on. Your job is to start slowly adding more fuel to her fire until it is raging to consume you.

Add variety, spontaneity, originality, and creativity in your lovemaking. If the bedroom is boring, try other locations and other times. Keep it consensual and private and unpredictable. Keep in mind that your feelings of love for each other and your desire, interest and ability to perform sexually will vary greatly at different times of your marriage.

Great expectations: your pregnant wife

How do you convince your wife of her beauty while she is pregnant? You need to remind her that the ultimate expression of her femininity is in the pregnant state. Since you made her pregnant, your work is probably beautiful in your eyes. The more pregnant she becomes, the more completely feminine she is and the greater the turn-on.

> "The most important thing a father can do for his children is to love their mother."
>
> *Father Theodore Hesburgh*

By the way, it is perfectly safe to have relations while your wife is pregnant, the only stipulation being that you have the relations with your wife exclusively!

Particularly during pregnancy, when your wife's needs are greater than usual, the words of a wise clergyman make sense. He advised that rather than trying to analyze and understand our wives, we should focus on doing our job: giving her abundant attention, affection, appreciation, and being attentive to her needs.

As long as we conveniently used all "a's", don't underestimate the power of apologizing. Your ability to apologize for not doing "your job" will save you enormous amounts of upset and conflict. It is infinitely easier to apologize than it is to try and win the argument over the truth or debate over why your actions were not so bad.

In reality, it is often not your actions that get you into trouble but your lack of action. Forgetting to do your job, your honey-do list, a life cycle celebration such as an anniversary, etc., will get you in hot water fast.

When it comes to the small stuff, with your wife or others, it often pays to learn to say to yourself, "Who cares?" or "So what?" What will you win in fighting over issues of relatively small importance? Even if you think that you are right, bend rather than stiffen.

Remember, earlier in the book you downsized your ego. Your ability to bend is a much greater asset and virtue than being rigid, stiff, and digging in over every idea, discussion, argument, or perceived injustice. Bend, demote your ego and enjoy abundantly more peace in your life.

Marriage and continued dating.

Great parents can easily have a lousy or nonexistent marriage if they never have time alone. Regardless of the number of children you have, it is crucial that you continue to have time alone.

Think back to the time of courtship when your entire mind was completely focused on your future wife. You had the ability to eliminate all work problems, financial problems, posted eviction notices, and the burning building next to the restaurant where you were dining with your future wife. Your singular interest was her, not any of your responsibilities in life, but the joys you shared.

In fact, if you were smart, you likely had conversation that was skewed towards the more pleasant and upbeat aspects of your life. After all, aren't people more interested in others that are happy, successful, and optimistic?

When you do take the leap and go on a date night, think about how you behave and keep your concentration directed on your wife. Here's a tip: I have found it easier to keep my eyes glued to my wife when I let her face the dining room while I face her with only the wall behind. It is too tempting for me to look around the room, scouting for familiar faces and hoping to be seen. It is nearly irresistible to pass up the opportunity to catch a good customer for some spontaneous unplanned schmoozing when they pass by your table.

If you capitulate to your desire to schmooze with others, appreciate that your wife is not blind. She will notice that she is only a part of your agenda. Remind yourself that she is the reason you are out. Hide from the rest of your social group on your date nights. You will quickly remember why you married.

Similarly, consider taking a couple's trip out of town without kids, just you and your wife. Your time together may help your children notice that married adults make time for each other, love each other, and value time alone. Chances are, your kids are going to model their adult lives after yours. The best way you can ensure that your children have a great marriage is to show them the way that you have made your marriage a life-long shared journey.

No doubt there are some of you who are truly unable to leave town. You may have children with special needs or you may have financial restraints. You may still be able to make a steamy date at lunchtime. Make your day and her day by meeting at a local hotel or motel for a romantic lunch break. An out-of-the-ordinary date such as lunchtime love making at the hotel will be remembered for a long time. Don't be tempted to fall into the trap of thinking what a waste of $100 the hotel was. It was a bargain compared to the cost of the jewelry you would have to buy when she complains that you never give any sign of your love, affection, or desire to listen to her anymore.

Jealousy can be very helpful.

Remember the kid in your high school class that was brilliant, handsome, courteous, and a great athlete? All of us have felt some level of jealousy towards a person with all of those attributes.

Now recall friends that have wonderful relationships with their wives. Instead of using the emotion of jealousy in a negative way, use the emotion as a challenge to improve yourself. The jealousy of your friend's great marriage can take on the role of an inspiring type of admiration, -an admiration that fosters a driven desire to make yourself better in your marital relationship, ultimately improving your life. Relatedly, you can use the jealousy you feel when your wife takes notice of the handsome men portrayed in the movies or that present at gatherings to motivate you into keeping yourself reasonably fit and smartly dressed.

> "Coming together is the beginning.
>
> Keeping together is progress.
>
> Working together is success."
>
> *Henry Ford*

So, jealousy can be a good thing… if it results in your keeping yourself appealing to your spouse and improves the way you treat her. Remember to continue marketing yourself to your wife. Impress her with your worthiness of being her husband. Do a few sit-ups during commercials to make you more attractive to her. Say nice things about her.

Would you ever badmouth your best customer? How devastating would it be to your business if your best clients realized that you speak poorly of them? Always defend your wife. Talk up your wife; she will eventually hear how kindly you speak of her.

FAQ

Can I still have "Boys' Night Out" and still be a good husband?

The concept of men having time together is not in itself a bad thing. Whether you call it "fellowship" or "bonding" or whatever, it can even be a great thing. Even Fred Flintstone did his share of bowling nights and seemed able to function as a model caveman/husband. I believe the key is moderation, both in the frequency and level of activity involved.

I propose the following:

Nothing good ever happens after midnight.

More to the point, nothing good happens in a nightclub when you and your wife aren't together. I don't care what you say, if married people are out late drinking and dancing without the spouse, trouble is easy to find. There is nothing wrong with boys' night out or your wife having girls' night out. It's just that there is a turning point in a night out where you choose: will you bring the fun back home into the loving arms of your wife or will you follow it elsewhere into who knows what.

> the writer: [typing on computer] "I never had any friends later on like the ones I had when I was twelve. Jesus, does anyone?"
>
> *Stand By Me*

I have a friend whose wife always comes home from her night out in a very amorous mood. I say more power to them both! I just believe that at some point (and I'm assuming alcohol is involved) our sense of focus gets softened and we are very liable to getting misdirected. If you and your wife can establish a curfew for each other, where is the hurt in that?

As for strip clubs, some guys say that their wives don't mind them going there and "just looking." I say these ladies are either in denial, lying, or crazy. How could any sane person not mind you taking money and sticking it in some stranger's underwear? The only crazier person is you, for taking that money out of your marriage and being the one to put it there.

Don't kid yourself that you are a handsome stylish stud when that woman is only going to be there as long as you keep feeding dollars into her bikini strap. Face it, many of us are just plain old geeks—even if, thanks to the beverages you're drinking, you are thinking you're a chic geek.

Remember, the performers are far more interested in Alex Hamilton, Andrew Jackson, and U. S. Grant than in you; when you stop placing them in her thong, she'll be gone. And while she's doing her dance, she is likely looking off into space, making a grocery list of what she needs to pick up on the way home after work.

Let's think about this from a scientific perspective. Laboratory rats can be taught to push on a bar and get a pellet of food. If the food stops coming, the rats eventually stop pushing the bar. This is called extinction of the behavior. Like a lab rat, guys get a positive stimulus when an attractive woman is undulating in front of them. To prolong this event, the response is to give the woman more money. Eventually, you realize that the excitement will not escalate any further (legally) and the food pellet loses its luster.

If those lab rats start getting shocked instead when they push the bar, a negative reinforcement, they stop MUCH faster. For guys, having no money is definitely a negative reinforcement. Next time you are in one of these places, look around. Look for the SHOCK on some poor sucker's face when he realizes that he spent everything, even his Taco Bell money! In fact, look around and see the dumb expression on most guys' faces there. Is that who you want to be?

As long as we are on the topic of drinking with the guys, let me ask you a question. In your long and storied drinking career, how many times have you ever arisen the morning after a drinking night with the guys, or with anyone, and said to yourself, "I wish I had consumed one more drink last night. If I had swallowed one more drink, last night would have been perfect." If you have had that conversation with yourself, you are the first I have met! Please send me your autograph. You are amazing. Every one else I've met snickers and remembers the mornings when they wish they had imbibed a lot less.

Don't the "bad guys" get all the chicks?

Why do bad guys get so much attention? They draw interest because they display abundant confidence and are not ordinary. Some world leaders, (George W. Bush, for example) are notorious for something that bad boys are also known for: swagger. But in real life cockiness, arrogance, condescension, and disregard for laws and ethical behavior are counterfeits.

> "Don't worry that children never listen to you; worry that they are always watching you."
>
> *Robert Fulghum*

Go for the real thing. The confidence I am referring to comes from your application of devotion to committing yourself to her. By mastering and subduing that part of you that wants to follow Mr. Hamhock, you become more self assured and bolster your inner strength. This strengthened inner constitution and commitment to your wife and only to your wife takes on the form of confidence. Confidence in your knowledge that you are THE MAN for your woman. That form of confidence lets her know that you can be a successful breadwinner, father, husband, and family leader. Understand the feeling of security a woman possesses when she sees that her man is confident.

Consider how you would feel if the surgeon to whom you were entrusting your life did not have confidence that he could perform the procedure well. If you were foolish enough to stay with that surgeon you would be terrified as you were being wheeled into the operating room to receive your anesthetic. Better not to place your life in the hands of such a man!

Many find that being an interesting person also helps in building confidence. Interesting people have an ability to pursue lifelong learning and hobbies. Those with interests outside the box—the TV box that is— already stand out from the couch-potato crowd, both to others and to themselves. Before obsessing with being an interesting person, keep in mind that it is much more important to be an interested person than interesting. Trying to publicize your status as interesting can be arrogant and a turn off.

Think about it: you can have confidence, be interested, be interesting and remain a good guy, too.

What is the worst thing that even good husbands tend to do?

Even the best guys tend to forget the important dates. Let's not try to figure out why this happens, let's just keep it from happening. The following is hopefully a solution for those of us who are "calendar-challenged."

Write your important dates down below and tear the page out. Then enter these dates in your computer calendar, cell phone, paper calendar, and to-do list. Then lock the original document in a safe deposit box to fall back on in case all the reminders are lost. Do NOT ask your wife to remind you of these dates.

First Date (first kiss): _____

Date you proposed: _____

Wedding Anniversary: _____

Sweetest Day: 3rd Saturday in October

Her birthday: _____

Valentine's Day: February 14

Mother's Day: 2nd Sunday in May

A note about Mother's Day: Okay, I know and she knows that she is not your mother. She may even despise the times that you call out "Mommy Mommy Mommy, more desserts please!" Regardless of whether you think she finds it important that the young children buy or make her a Mother's Day gift, make sure it's done.

Take the children to the store and have them pick out the gifts. They can also make the card. If you decided that you and your wife were going to practice with a pet for a few years before having children, no problem. Purchase a gift on behalf of the dog and give it to your wife. She will be grateful.

Of course, your awareness of these dates is only half the battle. Next, you have to be able to DO something to recognize them with your spouse. The most obvious way is with a gift.

The purpose of a gift is to express your love. The most meaningful gifts therefore do not require any useful function. You have already learned that women are different than men. She values jewels, flowers, and notes because they are your way of meeting her need to feel your gratitude in a form that is important and meaningful to her and only her. She realizes that these items have no function other than to serve as a means for you to spend your hard-earned money on stuff that is a total waste, serves no purpose, and can never be sold, traded, or put to use. Your wife will appreciate that you bought the items for her all the more so because of their uselessness.

Why the emphasis on the word you? Because YOU must do the shopping, buying, and wrapping in order for the gift to have meaning to your wife. Your wife has a special place in her brain that allows her to discern whether the gift was picked up and bought by a staff member from the office or chosen and bought by you. The point of the gift was for you to express your love and appreciation, which means that you must shop. This is even more important if she knows that you hate to shop and often get lost in the mall when you do and then when finished cannot find your car in the parking lot. If the babysitter or the children's grandparents take them shopping, your wife will figure that out. Your wife knows everything. She is a better detective than you can ever dream to be.

> "What counts in making a happy marriage is not so much how compatible you are, but how you deal with incompatibility."
>
> *Leo Tolstoy*

No amount of accessorizing can substitute for your personal involvement. By doing it yourself, you give her the most incredibly valuable gift in the world, the gift that all husbands can afford: your time, interest, attention, affection, and gratitude. She likes those gifts as much as you might like Super Bowl tickets or a super duper lightweight weed eater. Truth be told, she will likely value your presence as much as your presents. Your presence at the store is a requisite for all presents you purchase for her.

The fact that you did the shopping is important, but it's not the only factor. Homer Simpson bought his wife, Marge, a bowling ball inscribed with the name "Homer." You'll need to do better than that!

Always choose a gift for her based on HER personality, likes, etc. Some women, contrary to what TV and magazines would have us believe, do not give a hoot about jewelry or flowers. All women are not the same. If women bought into the media, you'd get an electric razor for every occasion. Make it clear that you put some thought into your gift, that you know your woman. In actu-  ality, this is more important to her than the gift itself. If you give the florist a list of dates and your credit card number, after getting the same thing with the same message three or four times in a row, the gesture will symbolize your laziness rather than your sweetness. Time spent wrapping the gift will further demonstrate your intent to please her. Unwrapped presents that are otherwise appropriate lack the luster and polish that reflects the high priority you placed on recognizing and honoring her with a gift.

TROUBLESHOOTING

What comes to mind when you think about problems in a marriage? The most obvious has to be arguments, i.e. "fightin'".

If you are ready to start an argument with your spouse….

Think again before you go to battle with your spouse. It is always much easier to start the war than it is to get out of the war. Remember Vietnam, Iraq, and the movie, The War of the Roses. Once you initiate the argument, fight, or major disagreement, words and actions are said that cannot be retracted. The act of heading down the warpath makes reconciliation much harder than it would have been had you tried to solve things peacefully.

I've been taught a fascinating point about arguments. Nobody wants to lose an argument because that makes them the loser. On the other hand, you also wouldn't want to married to a loser, either. Therefore, any marital dispute lends an outcome that renders a winner and loser, and you will be a loser either way be definition or by association.

So if there is a burning issue between you, why not first try gently broaching to your wife the issues that bother you? Initiate the conversation before she repeats the behavior and compounds your frustration.

But good criticism needs preparation. Before offering a criticism, your love for her must be clear, not concealed under a mound of anger and frustration. How else should she understand that you are making an attempt to strengthen your marital bond with her? It is not fair to her if you allow your upset or anger to build as she perpetuates some actions that you find disturbing. It's your job to steer yourselves towards a discussion rather than drift into a fight.

Avoid the temptation to tell your friends or family about the problem. They can only complicate the issue, not resolve it. Only your wife can make things better, so talk to her and her only. You can't change her personality or the way she is wired but you can resolve issues that you choose to discuss with her. She is not perfect but, guess what? You aren't either.

Name calling and arguments…

So you heard "Sticks and stones can break your bones, but words will never hurt". I believe that line is absolutely wrong. Most physical injuries eventually heal, but injuries caused by hurtful words may never do so. Once the hurtful words are let loose, they can never truly be unsaid.

I was once told the story of a person haunted by unkind words he had said. He searched far and wide to find counsel on how to retract his statements, and so at last came to a great wise man.

> "Marriage is one long conversation, checkered with disputes."
>
> *Robert Louis Stevenson*

The sage said that they first had to go through an exercise before he could teach him how to retract his words. The sage had him hold his hand out, which he then filled with salt. The sage then told the man to throw the salt as far as he could. The little grains of salt scattered all over. The sage then told the man to go and pick up all the salt that he had thrown.

The man realized that just as he couldn't possible find all of the salt and take it back, so he could never find and take back all of the words that were thrown out.

Whether you gossip about her or say harsh words to her face, hurtful words are very difficult to retract.

It is much harder to forget harsh words than it is to remember them. She may never forget the gnarly words you throw at her in the heat of battle. Even if she tries, the mean-spirited language will continue to echo in her mind.

While we appreciate that words can be more harmful than physical pain, don't take that as any kind of license to cause physical hurt. Use of physical force against your spouse is never acceptable.

Important side-note about HER family…

You thought that I would never get to the topic. Hating the in-laws is a classic cliché in the relationship world, but is not to be encouraged nor is it universal. Sometimes, though, there's a really good reason not to like them. However, the part that is taboo is badmouthing the in-laws, especially expressions of your dislike in front of your wife. Although she may have made bad comments regarding her parents, don't join in. Now or at some point in the future, she will remember that she is "one of them". After all, she is genetically related to them, not you. They made her. She is probably similar to them (or eventually will be) in more than one way. In fact, if she does not seem like them at all, just wait a couple of decades and compare again.

If there is ever a time not to jump in with your wife in reinforcing her opinion, it is with regards to her parents and family in general. Not to say that you have to disagree with her. Rather, your remarks should be tempered and lack the same bite they may have when taking her side on other issues. Any unkind words that you let slip regarding her family may come back to haunt you at a later date.

Bonus advice regarding YOUR family…

In times of strife in your marriage, it is second nature to look to someone for validation of why things aren't your fault. For many, family members can provide that shoulder to cry to and lean against. Remember this: If something your spouse does is nearly unforgiveable, but you eventually can find it in your heart to forgive, don't count on family to be so understanding. (This does not include violence.)

For example, if your mate burns your clothes in the driveway in a fit of rage, you may eventually celebrate with some new duds, but your momma may never again see her the way you do. Improprieties against their flesh and blood can make future family get-togethers a very uncomfortable thing. This may sound odd, but your ability to kiss and make up later is all that matters, and it only gets harder if a smooth future requires a lot more forgivers.

> "Bad marriages
> don't cause
> infidelity;
> infidelity causes
> bad marriages."
>
> *Frank Pittman*

The scoop on having an argument:

Sometimes, as Patrick Swayze said in Road House, you "be nice until it's time to not be nice." Whether you are right or you are wrong, the response is remarkably similar. We tend to get defensive when in an argument and tend to blurt out misdirected assignments of blame. NEVER blame her anger on her hormones. (Speaking of never, NEVER tell your wife she is fat!)

The list of "nevers" is endless, but here's what you CAN do:

Turn off the TV.

Put the newspaper down.

Look at her in the eyes.

Listen to her very carefully.

Lean forward towards her to demonstrate your interest.

Repeat her claims against you to assure her that you listened.

Ask her if she can think of anything else.

Sometimes, the last statement is the one that packs the most punch from an angry person. Consider that she probably has been building up to the explosion for quite some time and the current incident may not have provoked the outburst.

Empathize with how she must feel. Try to recall how you felt when you perceived that you were similarly wronged or dissed.

You must reach down and find at least a particle of truth in what she has claimed. Apologize…then make some strategies for avoiding a repeat performance.

The kiss and make up stage can be a big payoff. Avoid playing the defense attorney when she makes allegations against you. Do not fight back by recalling crimes committed in the past by her. To search and debate right now over what really happened and what was really said in the past is fruitless and will only make the conflict grow.

Fight fair and understand that it is possible to agreeably disagree. This method is actually applicable to any verbal conflict, whether it is your wife, a coworker, or your next-door neighbor (except for the kiss-and-make-up part). The hard part is not to respond emotionally and return the attack against the angry person.

IN CASE OF EMERGENCY

If you have intentionally come to this section, your marriage must be in dire straits. What now? Most important: do not attempt to return your malfunctioning marriage to the place of purchase. (Sorry, the owner's manual mentality kicked in again!) Truly, no manual can address the complexities of a marriage in mid-shipwreck. One thing you must do is try to step outside of yourself to see what part you are playing in the process. Are you the cause of the problem? Do you even want to fix it?

What NOT to do: Have an affair...

The sure fire way to destroy a marriage and to end any opportunity of reconciling is to start an affair. If you have a second lover, your wife does not have a chance to win the competition. Your girlfriend only sees you on dates. When your girlfriend meets you in the hotel during an affair, she is primped to the max; when you see your wife in the morning, she has not had the chance.

> "Marriage is popular because it combines the maximum of temptation with the maximum of opportunity."
>
> *-George Bernard Shaw*

In fact, when you come home from work, she may not be gussied up for you. Her weak excuse? She's been to the grocery to feed you, been to the dry cleaner to pick up your clothes for work, taking man's best friend to the vet for his annual shots, been to the school to read books to your first-grader's class, cleaned the vomit off the carpet from the four-year-old's most recent bout with the flu, met the cable guy at the house to repair the television service so you can watch the heavyweight boxing title fight tonight with your beer-guzzling and cigar chomping belching boxing buddies, and been to the doctor's office to have the stitches removed from her chin incurred from a fall while scraping the ice off your windshield before you went to work last Friday. And you dispassionately consider that she is not as fresh, well rested, made-up, and raring to go for hours of passionate, no-holds-barred, wild sex as your new love interest.

Remember, the girlfriend is auditioning for the new role as your exclusive woman. Chances are, she is on her absolute best game for you every time she is with you. She knows the dance and has determined she's not to be outdone by a wife.

Are you dumb enough to think that this is her first affair? If she does in fact land you, what makes you think she would be monogamous with you? Won't she go after another married guy if he seems to be a better deal than you? You cannot reconcile with your wife if you have a girlfriend. If you are married and have a girlfriend, drop this book. Actually, wait until you've read two more lines, then drop the book.

Next, drop the girlfriend. Work on your marriage with no distractions. (Okay, drop the book and come back when you're done.)

Now you can finish the book, then buy the book for all of your friends and send me a testimonial that I can place on the cover of my next one.

If the marriage is over, though, don't forget you'll need to keep a sense of self-respect and dignity. And the best way to do that is to preserve the dignity of your ex-spouse.

She deserves your respect. She was willing to marry you, care for you, take on your name, make children with your flawed gene pool and share a bathroom with you. Criticism of her when the marriage is over or ending is unfair and unnecessary. The only value in criticism is to build the relationship; it's ending now, and criticism has no place.

If there are children involved, then a different relationship will necessarily be formed to maintain the dual households for your kids. You must continue to be respectful to your ex. You cannot expect your children to show respect and honor their mother if you do not. If you have a criticism to offer your ex, preface it by articulating that the purpose of your remarks is to help the two of you move forward and build a better relationship in providing dual parenting for your children.

There may be a simple way to minimize the temptation to stray into actions that are counterproductive to a happy and lasting marriage. In so many areas of our lives— career, family, finances, hobbies and even marriages— we see some people that seem to find success without the same number of detours, distractions, and dead ends as others.

The successful people in every field seem to be able to avoid becoming derailed by having a sound and concrete vision of what they want in all areas of their life. They are so dedicated to realizing their vision that the temptations for short-lived pleasure are not as appealing. Their vision is their overriding desire; temptations lose their power to delude them.

You too must visualize your ideal with great clarity and focus, and then destructive fantasies will lose their attraction.

If you have already strayed…

Reading this book may have awakened a better man within you. One who is dedicated to righteousness and getting the full potential out of himself and his relationship. This catharsis may prompt you to come clean about a previous transgression to get a clean start.

Stop! If you blew it once and feel deep remorse, heed this book to help prevent a recurrence. If you feel overwhelmed with the desire to discuss your colossal screw-up or you are tempted once again, seek the counsel of clergy or a professional counselor. You need confidentiality; you can't count on that with a friend. Discussing your single, albeit huge, mistake may be too much for your wife to bear. It may result in the break up of the marriage. Why should she relieve you of the burden of your mistake? Why should she pick it up at all?

Remember, it is you that must learn the appropriate "R's": regret, remorse, repentance, repair, and regeneration of self. Most importantly, resist the temptation in the future. You truly deserve to be hard on yourself. You almost wrecked your marriage.

It is ok to remember your weakness for the rest of your life—it will help you not to do it again. Remembrance of the intense guilt, the anxiety of the sin, and of the possibility of being caught by people that care for you should help you battle the urge to stray. Simply put: don't do it again; just move on.

If you have had repeated affairs, you need the help of a professional and may need your spouse to be involved with the counseling. An expert may help you to use all the resourcefulness, cleverness, meticulous planning, and romantic inclination you invested in the other woman to start a new affair with your wife. She may keep you and give you another chance.

Impress her with the attributes that you put forward with the girlfriend. You have the ability to be a better person and a husband. You made the first step, recognizing the problem, buying the book, reading the book, and now developing your action plan.

What if your wife is the one that strays? If you truly love her, you will probably be able to forgive her. But there are two mutual requirements that you must insist upon: she must im-

> "New love is the brightest, and long love is the greatest; but revived love is the tenderest thing known on earth."
>
> *Thomas Hardy*

mediately break off all contact with her lover; and she must recommit to you. Perfection was not the prerequisite to being your wife; her love, devotion and commitment were. Those essential elements may still be present after adultery.

PRODUCT REVIEW

If you have muscled through this manual and are ready to put it up on a shelf, you are allowed to high five yourself for putting forth the effort. After all, "It's the thought that counts."

Not quite. While it is good and healthy to have good thoughts and good intentions, they are useful only if they lead to good deeds and good actions. Having good thoughts and intentions are a very good start, but useless if not implemented. Similarly, knowledge is good, but only if it is put to use in a positive and productive way.

Let me share an observation that is the product of many meetings and reading many self-help books: After all is said and done, a lot more is said or read than done.

> westley: "Hear this now: I will always come for you."
>
> buttercup: "But how can you be sure?"
>
> westley: "This is true love - you think this happens every day?"
>
> *The Princess Bride*

Make this book the exception. Now that you know that you will spend the rest of your life with your wife, why not implement the concepts and tools you've learned here? You're planning to spend the bulk of your adult life with her. Why not dedicate a concerted effort to making the marriage good? Or do you wish to endure pain and agony unparalleled by most mortals? Only a person as strong as an ox and a little bit dumber could survive!

On the other hand, you may be convinced that you intuitively have always known exactly how to be the wonderful husband that you think you are. Therefore, the manual has hopefully been funny and entertaining to you, but in no way useful.

Congratulations! You may be one of the few blissful people who really don't have any room for growth or improvement.

...Riiiiight!

Look hard into the mirror, or better yet, ask your wife how you are doing. There is an expression I used to describe myself early in my marriage. I too was a victim of the condition I now call "incompetent bliss." That is, I was one that knew so precious little about the topic that I didn't know that I didn't know. I was happy, temporarily, until I was told the truth.

Fortunately, my wife does not internalize well. She diagnosed my malady and told me to find a cure or find a new wife! Hence, incompetent bliss was cured and the book written for other infected men.

The problem with the mental state of incompetent bliss is that your spouse may not be sharing all the blissful feelings that you have. Worse yet, she may be afraid to tell you of her disappointment.

If she is sharing the bliss, you were meant for each other. Have a great life together!

This book was written with the intent to help the average guy organize his priorities and make his marriage better. If you understand every concept put forth in this book, you still will not benefit if you do not apply it. But since we have covered a lot of information, the best way to prime you for action is to review the main points:

Treat her like a queen

Let the head be in control of the heart and the hamhock

Instill creativity in your sex life

When in dispute, agreeably disagree

Be a gentleman and respect her privacy

The golden rule holds that we should treat others as we would like to be treated. If you can manage to live that, you can't do much better in life. No other saying better describes how mankind can live in harmony.

But marriage involves womankind, too. Since men and women are inherently different, perhaps the rule should be adapted to apply better to marriage. My wife loves gold. She also loves platinum! For the sake of a name, let's call this

"The Platinum Rule":

Treat your wife as SHE wants to be treated.

THAT is this book in a nutshell. Treat her as you want her to treat you, but then take it a step beyond that by realizing that how YOU want to be treated in a given situation may differ greatly with the way SHE wants to be treated.

It does very little good to treat her perfectly according to some expert's list of perfect husband must-do's . After all, you are serving your wife and her unique desires and wishes, not anybody else's vision of what a woman wants, and especially not your concept of what a woman should or does want. Think outside your own box and try to live in her moment instead of yours. If you can manage that, you're in!

Okay. Remember that visual from the beginning of the book? Where you're at the bar with your buddy? Well, it's closing time. Time not to hit the strip clubs and stagger home later with your tail between your legs. Time to say, "See ya!" to your buddy, go home, and work on being happy with your wife. Good luck and drive safely!

INDEX

Bibliography;

I am of the opinion that precious few, if any, of our thoughts are original. Rather we are deeply influenced by those with whom we spend time and by that which we read, see, and hear. A partial listing of my primary movers:

Teri German

Lisa Burke

Phyllis and Jerry DeVorkin

Mary Beth and Jerry Burke

Bonnie and Bill German

Elaine German

Rocky Balboa

Nissen Mangel

Manis Freedman: Various Audiotapes

Dennis Prager: Various Audiotapes

Aryeh Pamensky: 2003 live lecture, Dayton, OH

Boteach, Shmuley, *Dating Secrets of the Ten Commandments*. New York, Doubleday, 2000.

Boteach, Shmuley, *Kosher Adultery*. Avon, MA, Adams Media Corp., 2002

Boteach, Shmuley, *Kosher Sex: A Recipe for Passion and Intimacy*. New York, Doubleday, 1999

Leder, Steven Z, *More Money Than God*. Chicago, Bonus Books, 2003

Illustrations made better or created by Jenifer Schneider.

Cover and interior design by Jeremy Loyd
Illustrations by

EPILOGUE

By the way, I can't leave you without reviewing perhaps the most poignant quote of movie history, as told by Mitch (Billy Crystal) at his son's career day at school:

mitch robbins: Value this time in your life kids, because this is the time in your life when you still have your choices, and it goes by so quickly. When you're a teenager you think you can do anything, and you do. Your twenties are a blur. Your thirties, you raise your family, you make a little money and you think to yourself, "What happened to my twenties?" Your forties, you grow a little pot belly you grow another chin. The music starts to get too loud and one of your old girlfriends from high school becomes a grandmother. Your fifties you have a minor surgery. You'll call it a procedure, but it's a surgery. Your sixties you have a major surgery, the music is still loud but it doesn't matter because you can't hear it anyway. Seventies, you and the wife retire to Fort Lauderdale, you start eating dinner at two, lunch around ten, breakfast the night before. And you spend most of your time wandering around malls looking for the ultimate in soft yogurt and muttering "how come the kids don't call?" By your eighties, you've had a major stroke, and you end up babbling to some Jamaican nurse who your wife can't stand but who you call mama. Any questions?

City Slickers

Made in United States
North Haven, CT
16 July 2022

21452312R00033